Kids' Book of
Magic Tricks

Kids' Book of
Magic Tricks

• Michael Smith •

Watermill Press

Published in 1993 by Watermill Press.
Copyright © text and illustrations
The Five Mile Press Pty. Ltd., 1991, 1993
Produced for Watermill Press by
Joshua Morris Publishing, Inc.
Wilton, CT 06897 U.S.A.
in association with
The Five Mile Press Pty. Ltd.
All rights reserved.
Printed in U.S.A.

10 9 8 7 6 5 4 3 2 1

Contents

ABRACADABRA!

Please ask a parent to supervise when using appliances, needles, balloons, matches, raw eggs, hot tea, etc.

Introduction

You don't need any special skills (or elaborate equipment) to perform these tricks. Some of them may seem quite simple—once you've read how they're done. But remember your audience won't know the secret behind the trick, so they'll be mystified at your seemingly magical powers!

Once you've memorized a particular trick (and possibly had a practice run), you're ready to face your audience. But don't forget that *how* you perform the trick is almost as important as the trick itself.

Practice looking as if you're exerting incredible powers of concentration (for mind-reading tricks), try adding a dramatic flourish to your hand-movements, and master the art of distracting the audience's attention at the crucial moment.

Perhaps you'll be able to get hold of some magical-looking clothes—a dark jacket or dress—to which you can glue silver or gold stars. If you're really lucky you might be able to borrow a top hat and tails.

A magic wand is a very effective prop. You could make one by cutting off about 12 inches (30 cm) from the end of an old wooden dowel and painting it black, with white tips. Or you might be able to buy one from a magic shop.

And don't forget to throw in the odd "Abracadabra!" The rest is up to you. Have fun!

He/She

All tricks in this book are equally suitable for boys or girls. We have randomly used either the male or female personal pronoun throughout a particular trick to avoid the constant use of "he or she," "his or hers," etc.

✱ After you have cut the lady in half —
see page 20 — for some Magic Mending!

Mind-reader

Easy
Quite Easy
Quite Hard

Here's a great trick that's really simple to do.

You'll need:

A deck of cards

Ask a friend to choose fifteen cards from your deck.

Tell your friend to remember one of the cards she's chosen, but not to tell you which one it is. Then tell her that you're going to read her mind and tell her which card she's picked.

Deal the fifteen cards face up onto a table. Make three piles with five cards in each pile. Make sure you do it like this: put three cards on the table. Then put a card on top of the first one, then one on the second one, and then one on the third one. Then put the seventh card on top of the first pile, the eighth on the second pile, and the ninth on the third pile, and so on, until you've laid out all fifteen cards.

Ask your friend to watch you deal, and tell you which pile her card is in.

Pick up the cards, putting one pile on top of the other, and then deal out the cards again, laying them out in the same way as before. Ask her to tell you which pile her card is in now.

Do it a third time, and ask her to tell you which pile her card is in again. Then tell her to think about her card while you hold the pile with her card in it behind your back. Watch her face when you present the card she is thinking of!

The trick:

When you pick up the cards each time, put the pile with your friend's card in it in the middle of the two piles. After you've done it three times, your friend's card will always be the middle card in its pile. All you have to do is pick up the pile containing her card, and put it behind your back. Her card will be the third one from either end!

Remember:

The trick will only work if you deal the cards out as described above. If you make one pile, and then a second and then a third, the trick won't work!

Money-maker

✓ **Easy**
Quite Easy
Quite Hard

You'll need:

Six coins
*A piece of
double stick tape*

*Be careful with
this trick: if you
show it to your
parents, they may
decide that they
don't need to give
you an allowance
anymore!*

Next time you hear people say they can't
afford something, tell them that it's easy to
make money. You'll show them how.

Roll up your sleeves, and count five coins
onto the table. Let everyone see that your
hands are empty.

Cup your right hand on the edge of the table,
and sweep the five coins into it with your
other hand or a spoon or whatever you
like.

Close your hand over the coins, and say
the magic words. Then put the coins into
someone else's open hand so that they can
be seen and counted. There are now six!

I'm broke!

12

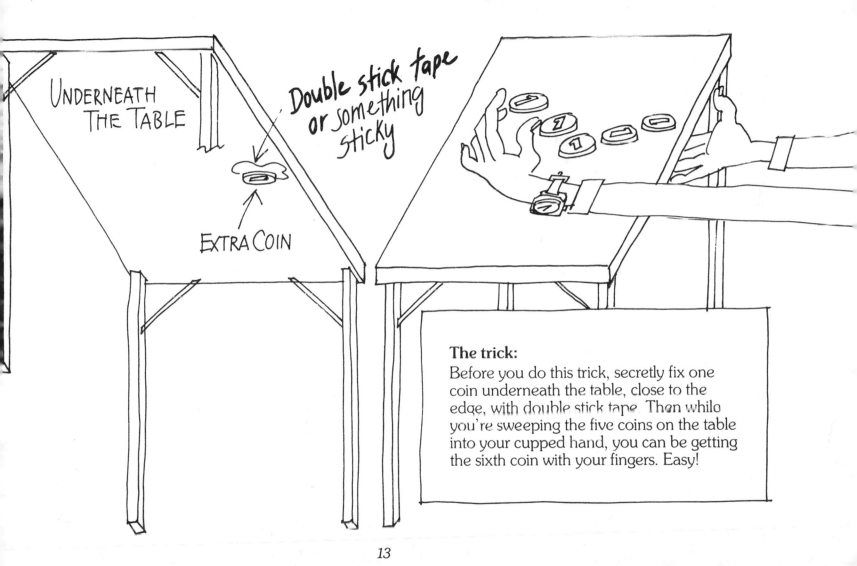

UNDERNEATH THE TABLE

Double stick tape or something sticky

EXTRA COIN

The trick:

Before you do this trick, secretly fix one coin underneath the table, close to the edge, with double stick tape. Then while you're sweeping the five coins on the table into your cupped hand, you can be getting the sixth coin with your fingers. Easy!

Magic Writing

Ever made invisible ink? Here's a way to make it, and a way to use it in a trick.

Easy
Quite Easy
Quite Hard

You'll need:
A lemon
Some paper
A toothpick
A toaster or lamp

Begin by acting mysteriously. Move very slowly around the table, and pretend to be hearing something.
Tell your audience that there's a ghost in the room. Ask if they can hear him.

Point to a place in the corner of the room, and tell them that you can definitely see something there (but of course there isn't anything there at all!).

Ask everyone if they can see the ghost. Someone will say that they can't. Then you can tell that person that you will prove it by asking the ghost to write something on the piece of paper that you put on the table for your next trick.

Call out loudly, "Whoever you are, prove to us that you really are a ghost! Write something on the paper on the table."

Pretend to watch while the ghost moves across the room to the table and writes on the paper.

Then watch the ghost walk away back to the corner.

Pick up the paper. Show everyone that it's blank. Then go over to the toaster and turn it on. Hold the paper over the toaster so that everyone can see, and slowly a message will appear in brown lettering.

The trick:

Beforehand, you have written the message on the paper using the toothpick as a pen and the juice from the lemon as ink. As the paper becomes warm, the "ink" will turn brown and the message will appear!

The Magic Cup

You can make a coin disappear with this trick— and then you can make it reappear again just as easily!

✓ **Easy**
✓ **Quite Easy**
Quite Hard

You will need:

A glass or plastic cup (one that you can see through)
Two sheets of white paper (they must be exactly the same shade)
Some glue
A coin
A handkerchief

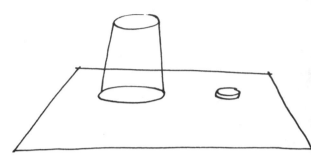

Ask a friend to give you a coin. Take the coin, and ask another of your friends to examine it closely to make sure that it is real.

Then explain that you can make coins like this disappear.

Place the coin on the sheet of paper and the glass beside it.

Make a fuss of shaking the handkerchief and showing your audience both sides of it. Then cover the glass with it.

Lift the glass with the handkerchief over it, and place it on top of the coin.

Wave your magic wand, say the magic spell, and then lift the handkerchief. The coin has disappeared!

Then tell the person who gave you the coin that she shouldn't be worried—you can bring the coin back just as easily as you made it disappear!

Drape the handkerchief over the glass. Wave the wand and say the magic words. Then lift the glass—and the coin is back!

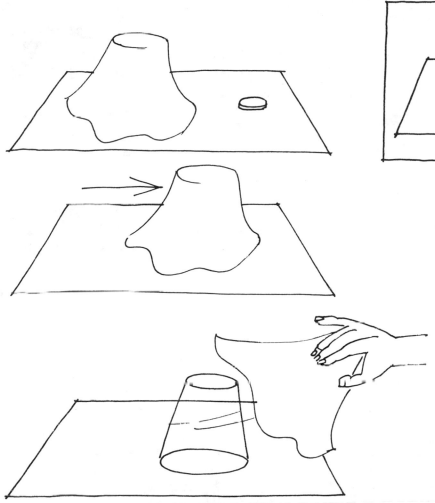

paper circle

glue

The trick:

You must prepare the glass beforehand as follows:

Turn the glass upside down on top of the first piece of paper, and carefully draw a circle around it with a pencil. Then cut the circle out, and glue it to the mouth of the glass.

If you do this properly, the circle should be exactly the same size as the mouth of the glass, so that when you place the glass upside down on the second piece of paper, no one will be able to see your cut-out circle.

When you place the glass on top of the coin, the paper covers it up so that it's invisible. Then it magically reappears when you lift the glass. Easy!

The Magic Rolling Ball

✓ Easy
Quite Easy
Quite Hard

You'll need:

A long piece of
string
A small plastic
ring
A ball
A table with a
cloth on it

*Here's a trick that
will make
everyone totally
convinced that
you have magic
powers...*

COME!

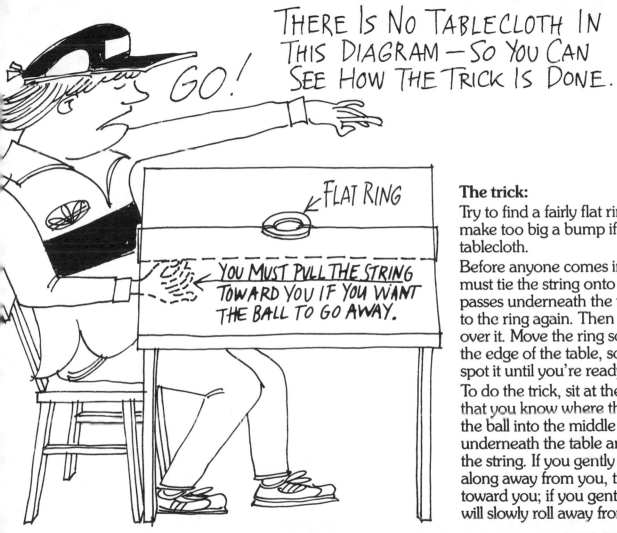

The trick:

Try to find a fairly flat ring, one that doesn't make too big a bump if you put it under the tablecloth.

Before anyone comes into the room, you must tie the string onto the ring so that it passes underneath the table and then back to the ring again. Then put the tablecloth over it. Move the ring so that it sits near the edge of the table, so that no one will spot it until you're ready to do the trick.

To do the trick, sit at the table. Make sure that you know where the ring is, and place the ball into the middle of it. Reach underneath the table and hold tightly onto the string. If you gently push the string along away from you, the ball will roll toward you; if you gently pull the string, it will slowly roll away from you!

19

Magic Mending

✓ **Easy**
Quite Easy
Quite Hard

This trick doesn't need too much equipment. Try it!

You'll need:

Two identical envelopes
Some glue
Two identical playing cards
Scissors

Tell your audience that you're going to do some magic mending.

Pick up a card and show the audience that it is perfectly normal. Then take the scissors, and cut the card in two.

Pick up the envelope and open it, turn it upside down, and shake it to show that there's nothing inside.

Put the two halves of the card inside, and seal the envelope.

Place the envelope on the table and say that you hope this works because you haven't practiced it before.

Pick up the envelope, slit it open, and peer anxiously inside. Look very worried, and slowly pull the card out—it's whole again!

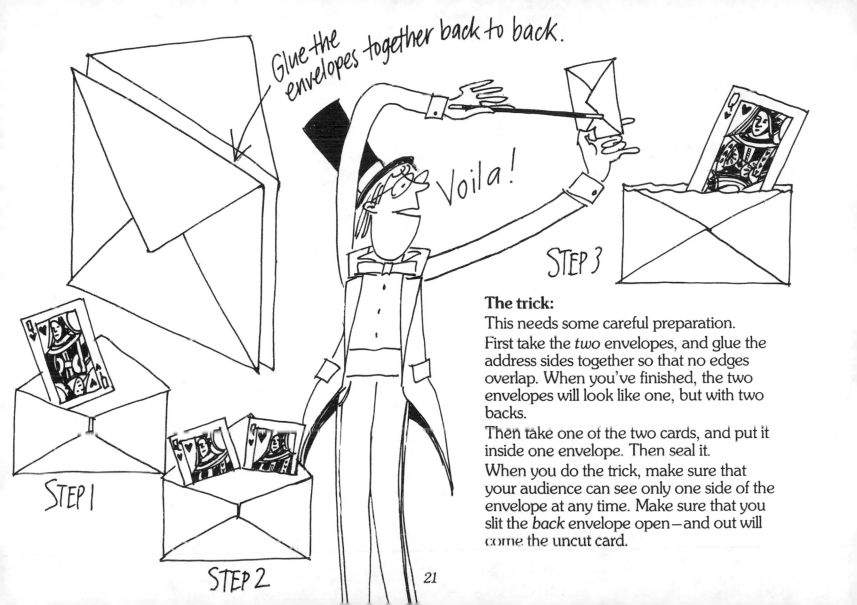

Glue the envelopes together back to back.

Voila!

STEP 1

STEP 2

STEP 3

The trick:

This needs some careful preparation.

First take the *two* envelopes, and glue the address sides together so that no edges overlap. When you've finished, the two envelopes will look like one, but with two backs.

Then take one of the two cards, and put it inside one envelope. Then seal it.

When you do the trick, make sure that your audience can see only one side of the envelope at any time. Make sure that you slit the *back* envelope open—and out will come the uncut card.

21

Card Telepathy

Easy
✓ **Quite Easy**
Quite Hard

This is a simple trick with a piece of apparatus that may take a little time to prepare— but it can be used again and again.

You'll need:

*A deck of playing cards
Scissors*

Hold the deck face down, and spread the cards out in the shape of a fan.

Ask one of the audience to pick any card and look at it with great concentration, but not to tell you what it is.

While she is studying her card, tidy up the cards you are holding and **turn the deck around.** Then fan out the deck again.

Ask the person to put the card back anywhere into the deck.

Tidy up the deck again, and then hold the deck behind your back. Tell the person to think about her card so that you can tell her which one it is. After a few moments, look worried, and ask her to concentrate harder. Then pull a card from the deck behind your back and show her —it's the card she was thinking of!

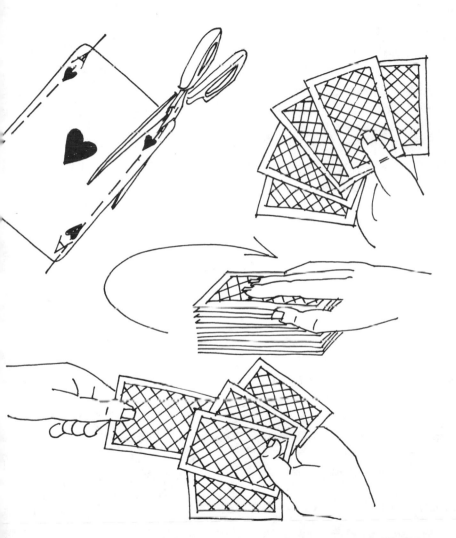

The trick:

For this trick you will need a specially altered deck, called a "tapered deck." A deck of cards like this is slightly narrower at one end than at the other. You can do this by taking each card and carefully cutting a little from each side, so that one end is slightly wider than the other. This is a long job, but the deck can be used for a lot of different tricks. You can get specially made decks like this from stores that sell magic tricks.

Once you have your tapered deck, this trick is simple!

First make sure that all the cards are the right way around, with all the narrow edges at one end. When you tidy up the cards, and then turn the deck around, it's easy to feel out the card your friend has put back in the deck. It's the only one that is wider than the rest at one end!

The Mystery Toothpick

✓ Easy
Quite Easy
Quite Hard

You'll need:

*A cloth,
handkerchief, or
a napkin with a
hem
A felt pen
A box of toothpicks
A spare toothpick*

Ask someone from your audience to open the box of toothpicks, take out one toothpick, and mark it with the pen.

Open the handkerchief or napkin, and wave it to show that there is nothing hidden in it. Wrap it around the toothpick.

Let someone from the audience feel the toothpick inside the napkin. Then ask her to break it in half while it is still inside the napkin.

You take back the napkin, wave a hand over it, and say a magic spell. Then you shake it open. The toothpick with the mark on it falls out unbroken!

Show it to the person who marked the original toothpick, and ask her if it's the same one. It is!

The trick:

Beforehand, slide the spare toothpick into the hem of the napkin, out of sight.

When you fold the napkin with the marked toothpick inside, make sure that you keep track of the part of the hem with the spare toothpick inside, and try to keep it in the middle of the folded bundle. That's the one that you will get the member of your audience to break in half—not the marked one!

PUSH THE TOOTHPICK INTO THE HE[M]

DON'T FORGET WHERE YOU PUT IT!

Four Naughty Boys

Easy
Quite Easy
Quite Hard

You'll need:

Your tapered deck (see "Card Telepathy").

Tell the audience that the jacks in the deck of cards are really naughty; they are always getting into trouble and hiding. Luckily you always know where to find them, and this keeps them in order. You're going to show your audience just how easily you can do this.

Show someone in the audience the deck face up, and pull all four jacks out of the deck one at a time. Each time you find one, wag your finger at the card and frown hard at it before laying it face up on the table in front of you. Let your "victim" look through the deck to see that there are no more jacks in there.

Replace the jacks and then shuffle the cards. Hold them behind your back. Then one at a time pull four cards from behind you, and lay them face down on the table in front of you.

Turn the cards over one at a time—they are the four jacks!

Let your "victim" have another look at the deck to make sure that they really are the jacks from the deck.

Say to your audience, "Now you know why the jacks don't act up when I'm around!"

The trick:

It's easy with your tapered deck. Before you put the four jacks back you turn the deck around. Your will be able to feel the four cards when you hold the deck behind your back, and you'll be able to pull them out very easily.

The Magic Shape-Guessing Game

✓ **Easy**
Quite Easy
Quite Hard

Looking for another trick to demonstrate your amazing mind-reading powers? Try this one!

You'll need:

*A table
Six shapes cut from cardboard or paper—a circle, an x, a triangle, a square, a five-pointed star, and a hexagon
A pencil
A sheet of paper*

These lines are not drawn on the table—but you knew that already.

SQUARE

You explain that you will once again demonstrate your amazing powers of mind-reading.

You call up one of your friends, and ask him to help out. Then you go out of the room. While you're away, your assistant shows the shapes to the audience, and asks them to choose which one they want you to guess. Once they have decided, he asks someone to put the shapes in a heap on the table. You then come back in, and after a moment or two spent concentrating, you draw the shape on the piece of paper.

You hand it to someone in the audience, and it's the correct one!

The trick:

As with many good tricks, you have to prepare it beforehand with your assistant.

Each one of the shapes has something to do with a number: the circle has *one* side to it, the x is made of *two* lines, the triangle has *three* corners, the square has *four* corners, the star has *five* points, and the hexagon has *six* sides.

The secret is that beforehand, you and your assistant imagine the table top divided up into six parts, representing the six shapes, in the above sequence. When you come back into the room, your assistant casually leans one hand against the part of the table that signals a particular shape—and that tells you what shape everyone chose!

27

Magic Numbers

Think of a number
Double it
Add 10
Take away 4
Add 2
Halve it
Take away the number you first thought of
The answer is 4!

Here's another one.

Think of a number
Add 6
Multiply it by 2
Add 4
Halve it
Add 3
Subtract 5
Subtract another 6
Subtract the number you first thought of
The answer is zero!

✓ **Easy**
Quite Easy
Quite Hard

Here's a trick to try out on a friend. It never fails—provided you do the math correctly!

The trick:

It's easy, provided you follow these three simple rules.

1. Always make sure that you make your friend take away the number he first thought of right at the end.

2. Keep track of the numbers you add and take away.

3. If you ask him to multiply by a number (doubling it, or times three), make sure that you get him to divide by the same number later on (halve it, or divide it by three).

Try it with a few different sums; it works every time!

Family Fun

Easy
Quite Easy
Quite Hard

Here's a trick with numbers that works like "Magic Numbers."

THREE

Tell your friend that you can tell her how many cousins she has if she tells you how many aunts and uncles she has.

Let's say she has 4 aunts and 2 uncles. That's a total of 6.

Ask her to work out the following sums in her head:

Take the number of aunts and uncles and double it (12)

Then add 3 (15)

Multiply that number by 5 (75)

Add all the cousins (say she has 3) to that number (78)

Take away 15 (63)

Ask her what number she got as an answer. Tell her she's got 3 cousins! Watch her face.

The trick:

This is another simple number game. You must remember the number of aunts and uncles. The *first* number in her answer will probably be the one she gave you – the aunts and uncles. If it's not, subtract the number of aunts and uncles from that number. The remaining numbers represent the number of cousins.

The Magic Answer

$$7\ 8\ 2\ 4$$
$$\text{add } 7+8+2+4=2$$
$$7824-21=7803$$
$$7+8+0+3=18$$
$$1+8 \quad \text{Always } 9$$

✓ **Easy**
Quite Easy
Quite Hard

Here's a trick for someone who really likes math!

You will need:
A piece of paper
An envelope
A pen

Before you begin, write a number on a piece of paper. Seal it in an envelope.

Tell your audience that you are really magic, because you can tell the answers to problems beforehand. Explain that the answer to the next problem is in the envelope.

Next get someone from the audience to write down any four digits. (Let's say the person chooses 7824.)

Add these digits together $(7+8+2+4=21)$.

Subtract the answer to that sum from the original number $(7824-21=7803)$.

Add those numbers together $(7+8+0+3=18)$.

Add those two numbers together $(1+8)$.

Open the envelope. Both answers are the number 9!

The trick:

The magic number 9 will *always* be the answer to this trick, no matter what your audience chooses. Weird? Or is there an explanation?

Dotty Dominoes

Easy
Quite Easy
Quite Hard

For this trick you'll need a set of dominoes, a cloth, and the magic skills of a master magician...

Put all the dominoes on the table, face down, and ask someone from the audience to choose one. Then ask her to cover the rest with the cloth so that you can't see them. Next tell her to look at the domino and concentrate on it so that you can get a clear image of it in your own mind.

Look worried: the image isn't coming through very clearly. To help her exercise her mind properly, she will have to do some calculations with the numbers on the domino.

Tell her to look at the highest number on the domino and multiply it by 5.

Add 7

Double the answer

Add the lowest number on the domino to it

Take away 14

Ask her for the answer. Suppose it's 42. The two figures that make up the answer will be the same as the two numbers on the domino: 4 and 2. Tell her the two numbers, and watch her amazement!

The trick:

This is another number game that works every time, provided the person you choose can do the math!

The Vanishing Kid

Tell your audience that you're going to make someone disappear.

Ask for a volunteer to come out of the audience.

Have her step into the box and crouch down so that you can close the lid.

Say the magic words. Slowly tip the box onto its side, toward the audience, but keep the lid closed.

Open the lid. There's no one there!

✓ Easy
Quite Easy
Quite Hard

You'll need:

*A very big cardboard box with a lid
A piece of tape
Some glue*

The trick:

Prepare the box beforehand. Cut around the bottom of the box on three sides and then bend the bottom upward, inside the box. Glue a piece of tape on the underside of this piece, for a handle. When the "volunteer" (who is secretly in on the trick) steps into the box, she's really standing on the floor. So when you tip the box forward, she can hold onto the handle and slowly pull the bottom back into place.

When you lift the cover, the box will be empty, and your volunteer will be crouching behind the box. If you stand close to the box all the time, your volunteer can hide behind the box and you.

Get a small person to be the volunteer, so that hiding is easier. You'll have to rehearse this trick a few times before you do it.

You can bring your volunteer back by closing the lid and slowly standing the box upright again!

A Mind-reading Assistant

Easy
Quite Easy
Quite Hard

This is a good trick for you to let your hard-working assistant do—let her amaze everyone for a change!

You'll need:
A deck of cards

When you begin this trick, shuffle the cards so that everyone can see that they are well shuffled.

Then get three people from the audience to pick out a card each, and to look at their card carefully, so that they can remember it.

Then hold out the deck, and get your "victims" to put the cards back into the deck.

Hand your assistant the cards. Stand behind her and make some magic passes over her head with your hands, while telling your "victims" to think hard about the cards they have chosen.

One by one your assistant picks the correct cards!

MAGIC SPELL

34

The trick:

Before you begin the trick, turn the bottom card face up. When you shuffle the deck, make sure that you don't move the bottom card from the bottom.

Just before you hold out the deck for the "victims" to put their cards back, you secretly turn the deck over. The three cards are pushed back into the deck, but they are the other way around.

All that your assistant needs to do is to look through the deck for cards that are the wrong way around! Of course she will have to do this carefully so that no one sees the cards, or they will spot how the trick is done.

Mind-reading the Card

✔ **Easy**
Quite Easy
Quite Hard

This is a simple trick that you can try on a friend.

You'll need:
A deck of cards

Shuffle a deck of cards and, without looking at them yourself, ask your friend to pick out any one of them.

Ask him to look carefully at the card, and try to make a picture of it in his mind.

While he is doing that, put the cards together, and lay them in your right hand, face down. Hold your right arm out to the side. Then reach over with your left hand and pick up half the deck. With a theatrical sweep of your left arm, move it so that you are holding it out on the other side of your body. If you do this properly, you will have half the deck face down in one hand, and the other half face up in the other hand.

Ask your friend to place his card face down on the deck in your right hand.

With another theatrical sweep of your left hand, place the left hand pile of cards on top of the right hand one.

Now tell him that you will be able to find his card because you can read his mind.

Holding the deck face down, you turn over each card until suddenly you say, "This is the one." And you're right!

The trick:
This is very easy.

When you have split the pack in two, and you're holding both piles in your hands, glance quickly at the half that is face up (in your left hand). Make sure you remember the top card on that pile.

When you place the cards in your left hand on top of those in your right, the card you remembered will be next to the one that your friend chose.

As you lay out the cards one at a time face up, your friend's card will be the one after the one you remembered!

The real trick here is to make sure you haven't been spotted looking at the cards in your left hand...

This is the one

Double Mind-reading

Easy
Quite Easy
Quite Hard

This is a trick that you can do with two friends, although it will work with only one other person.

You will need:
A deck of cards

Put your deck of cards face down on the table in two piles. Say to your friends that you would like each of them to pick a card and look carefully at it. (One friend must choose from one pile, and the other friend from the other pile.)

Pick up one of the two piles, and ask one friend to put her card back anywhere she likes into the pile. Then pick up the other pile and do the same with the second friend.

Now you tell them that you know which card each of them has chosen.

Put both halves of the deck together in one hand. Then go through it carefully without letting your friends see the faces of the cards. Very quickly you pull out the two cards!

The trick:

For this trick you will need to prepare your deck beforehand. Separate the red cards from the black ones. Put all the red cards in one pile, and the black ones in the other.

While your friends are studying their cards, pick up one of the piles (say the red one). Be particularly careful to offer this red pile to the friend who took a card from the black pile. Then pick up the other pile (the black one this time) and do the same with the friend who picked a card from the red pile.

When you look through the whole pack, you will be able to see the cards that are different—and if you keep in your mind who took the red card and who took the black one, you will be able to tell which friend took which card!

The Magic Power

✓ Easy
Quite Easy
Quite Hard

Here's another trick that needs a friend to help you mystify your audience.

You will need:

*A die (one of a pair of dice)
A table high enough for you to sit under*

Get your audience to sit around the table. Tell them that they have to sit as close to the die as possible, as you need all the help you can from their minds to do this trick properly.

Explain that your maternal great-grandmother gave you special powers. You can always tell what number is shown on the die without even looking at it.

To prove it, you're going to sit under the table, and any one of them can roll the die on top of the table, where you can't see it. Someone rolls the die – and you call out what the number is – every time!

The trick:

This is an easy one, provided you've briefed a helper properly beforehand.

This is what you do: Your helper sits with one hand resting on his knee, out of sight. Whatever number appears on the die, he indicates with his hand – one is one finger, two is two fingers, and so on. If a six appears, he closes up his hand.

This is such a simple trick, yet it fools everyone!

The Unburstable Balloon

Easy
Quite Easy
Quite Hard

This trick is fun— watch everyone flinch while they wait for an explosion that just doesn't happen!

You'll need:

*Two balloons
Some sticky
transparent tape
A pin*

Produce two balloons and ask someone from the audience to choose one of them and blow it up for you. Once he has done that, question him closely. Is there anything unusual about the balloon? Is he sure it's perfectly normal?

Then give him a pin and tell him to stick it in the balloon without it bursting. Of course he can't. Once he sticks the pin in, the balloon goes pop.

You tell him that he just hasn't tried hard enough. Get him to blow up the second balloon and hand it to you.

Then you hold the balloon out and stick the pin into it—and the balloon doesn't burst!

The trick:

While the second balloon is being blown up, hide a piece of sticky tape in your fingers. (You should have cut a short length from the roll and stuck it by one corner to the table where your tricks are laid out.)

When you take the balloon, gently pat it, as if checking that it is blown up properly. In fact, you are sticking the tape onto the balloon, and patting it into place.

Then you stick the pin into the balloon— but through the sticky tape. If you do that it will not burst. Keep the pin in, or the balloon will deflate rapidly, and spoil your trick!

Matchbox Magic

✓ Easy
Quite Easy
Quite Hard

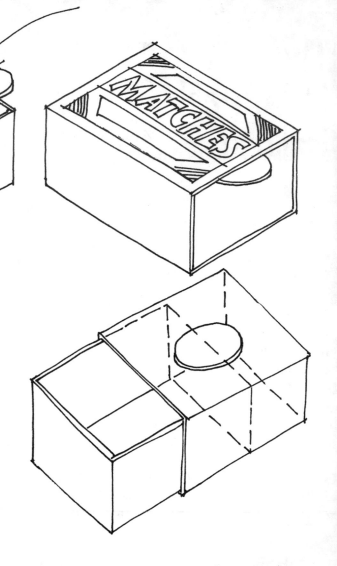

Here's a trick where you make something appear—not disappear.

You'll need:

*A matchbox
Two quarters*

Tell everyone that you are going to make some money for yourself—in fact you're going to double your money with the help of your magic matchbox!

Show everyone the first quarter—let them have a good look at it. You can even hand it around, if you're sure they'll give it back!

Pick up the matchbox and turn it upside down to show everyone that it's empty. Then carefully place the coin inside the

40

half-open matchbox. Show them that it's inside, and that there's only one coin in there. (You can even take the coin out again and show them it if you like.)

Shut the lid, wave a hand over the closed box, and then give it to someone to open. There are two quarters inside!

The trick:

As with most magic tricks, it takes some preparation beforehand to make things work.

Slide the second quarter between the top of the box and the back of the drawer. Then carefully open the drawer halfway, sliding the coin in at the same time. If you've done it correctly, the drawer will be half-open with the second quarter held out of sight between the top of the box and the back of the drawer.

When you close the drawer, the coin will drop into the box, and join the other coin that you have just placed there. To make sure that the trick works properly, hold the box with your finger around the back so that it can push the coin inside if it happens to slide out with the drawer.

Mind-reading Blindfold

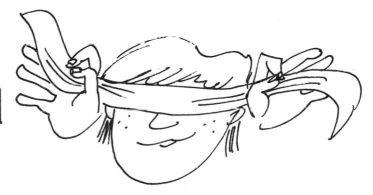

✔ Easy
Quite Easy
Quite Hard

This trick needs the help of an assistant who is in on the trick. Together you can mystify your friends.

You'll need:

Some cloth for a blindfold

First of all, show your blindfold to your audience. Let them see that it does not have any holes in it. Then get someone from the audience to tie it on, and to make sure that you cannot see through it or around it.

Now call for someone from the audience to help you.

Tell everyone that you can tell what this person is thinking if she puts one hand on her head and talks to you, and that you'll prove this now.

Ask everyone to look through their pockets and find an object. You will ask your assistant to take one object at a time, hold it up, put her hand on her head, and then ask you what the object is.

You will be able to say what the object is, provided she keeps her hand on her head. Of course you do this every time!

The trick:

The person you call up from the audience has been carefully prepared beforehand, and then sits in the audience pretending that she doesn't know what is going to happen.

You train your assistant like this. You give a secret code for each common object you can think of. For example, the secret code for a pen is "right." Your assistant holds up a pen and says to you, "Here's one you'll never get right."

For a watch it might be "see." Your assistant will say, "Can you see this in your mind? I bet you can't."

For a ring it might be "looking." When you hear your assistant say, "You're not looking, are you?", you know it's a ring she's holding.

Watch out now – no peeking.

It's a Chinese wat

The Magic Thimble

Easy
Quite Easy
Quite Hard

You'll need:
*A handkerchief
Two thimbles,
different colors
(one should be
able to fit inside
the other one)*

*This is a really
simple trick that
will fool an audience
every time!*

Place one thimble inside the other, and put both onto the middle finger of one hand. Show the audience your finger, and then wave the handkerchief about in a mysterious fashion. Tell everyone that you are going to bewitch the thimble. Cover your hand and the thimbles with the cloth, and then say a magic spell. Lift the cloth off, and the thimble has changed color!

The trick:
Of course what has happened is that you took the top thimble off when you removed the handkerchief, leaving the bottom thimble on your finger!
If you practice this a bit, you should be able to "turn the thimble back to its original color," and then wave the handkerchief mysteriously again at the end of the trick—but don't drop the top thimble while you're holding the handkerchief!

Blackbirds

✓ **Easy**
Quite Easy
Quite Hard

Try this one on younger brothers or sisters. It's really simple, but they'll never guess how it's done!

You'll need:

Two small stickers or two pieces of sticky paper (they should be about the size of your fingernail)
Sticky tape

Put one of the stickers on the middle fingernail of your right hand, and one on the middle fingernail of your left. You may need to secure them with sticky tape.

Make your hands into fists, with the middle finger sticking out. Tap the two fingers on the table and sing:

Two little blackbirds
Sitting on a wall
One named Peter
One named Paul
Fly away Peter
Fly away Paul
Come back Peter
Come back Paul.

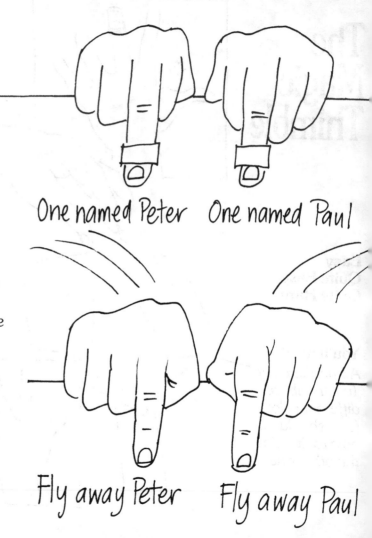

One named Peter   One named Paul

Fly away Peter   Fly away Paul

44

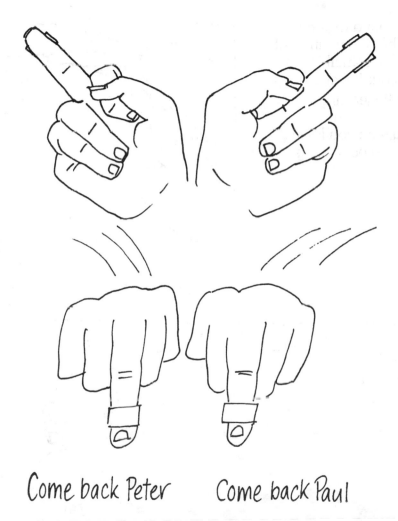

Come back Peter   Come back Paul

As you say "Fly away Peter," lift your left hand in a flying motion, bringing your extended finger back on the table—the sticker has gone! The same happens with your right hand as you say "Fly away Paul." Then, as you say "Come back Peter," you make your left hand fly up and land on the table once more—but this time "Peter" is back! The same happens with "Paul" on the right hand.

The trick:

The secret behind this simple trick is that when you say "Fly away Peter" (and the sticker disappears), you tuck your middle finger into your fist and extend your first finger. Then, as you call out "Come back Peter," you once again extend your middle finger with the sticker on it. The same goes for "Paul," and the right hand!

The Two-finger Trick

Bring one finger of each hand together horizontally about 2 inches (5 cm) in front of your nose. Stare hard at something in the distance just above your fingers.

Then slowly move your fingers apart a little. Look at the spot where your fingertips were touching, and you'll see something like a short sausage floating in the air in front of you.

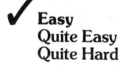

Easy
Quite Easy
Quite Hard

Here's a simple trick that everyone in your audience can do. It's a good one for a starter.

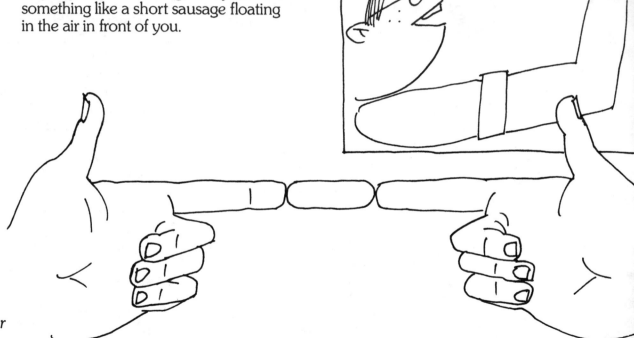

The Thumb Chop

Easy
Quite Easy
Quite Hard

This is a simple trick that can be made really exciting with some ketchup.

You will need:
A ruler
Some ketchup in a jar

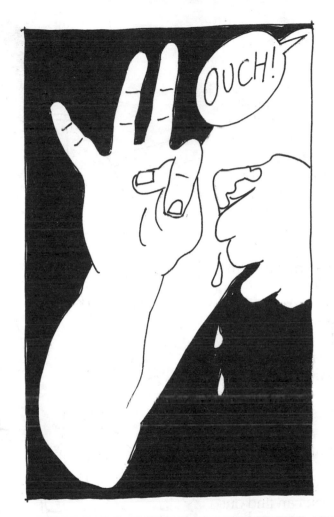

Tell your audience that if you concentrate hard, you can conquer pain. So good are you that you can even chop off a thumb with a ruler, and still smile!

You turn your back on the audience, and pretend to saw hard at your thumb, while you secretly dip the top knuckle of the same thumb into the ketchup.

Then turn around, smiling grimly, and show your audience that you really have cut it off. The messier you can make the ketchup, the more realistic it will look!

The trick is to hold your hands correctly when you turn around. Bend both your thumbs at the top joint and put them together. Then wrap a finger around the "top" of your severed thumb to hide the joint.

Lift the top thumb off the bottom one, and it will look just as if you've cut it in half!

Practice this in a mirror a few times beforehand. Remember, it has to look real to the people watching—not to you! The mirror will help you see what it looks like to them.

A Weight-lifting Team

✔ **Easy**
Quite Easy
Quite Hard

This looks like magic, although there's no real trick in it.

You'll need:
Five friends
A chair

For this trick, have one of your friends sit in a chair. Tell the others to stand around the chair, and clasp their hands together with the first fingers pointing outward.

Two people put their first fingers under the seated person's armpits, and two others put their first fingers under his knee joints; then all four try to lift him up in the air.

Of course they can't.

But you tell them that you can make them super-strong. And this is how.

Get them to place their hands in a pile on top of the person's head, and press downward while you say the magic spell. They should keep doing this for as long as it takes for you to count slowly to 20.

Then they take their hands away, and *immediately* try to lift the person again, with two fingers each.

Magically, they can do it this time—and very easily!

Why can they do it? See if you can find out.

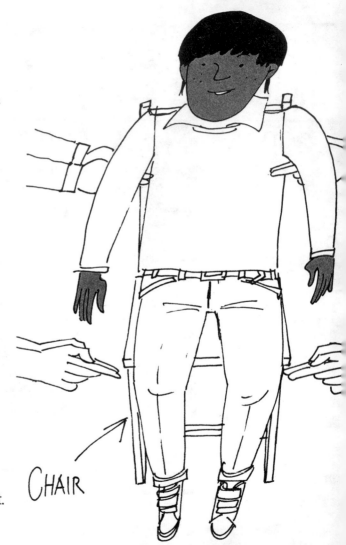

CHAIR

Bewitched Arms

✓ **Easy**
Quite Easy
Quite Hard

Here's another trick that unlocks mysterious forces in the body!

PRESS AS HARD AS YOU CAN

WALL

Ask a friend to stand sideways to a wall and very close to it. Tell her to press her arm as hard as she can against the wall, as if trying to raise her hand up above her head, while you bewitch her arm. Walk to and fro muttering your magic spell while secretly you count up to fifty, slowly. Then ask your friend to come away from the wall, and relax her arm.

She will be amazed at what happens, as the arm lifts itself away from her body without her doing anything!

You can make this trick even more effective by getting your friend to stand in a narrow doorway and press *both* arms outward at the same time.

Bewitched Knees

Easy
Quite Easy
Quite Hard

Here's another body trick. Can you find out how it works?

Bet a friend that you can bewitch him so that he will not be able to lift his right foot from the ground.

Tell your friend to stand sideways very close to a wall, so that all of the left side of his body is touching it—from his foot through to his shoulder.

Say the magic spell, and then tell him to lift his right foot. He just can't!

This trick can, of course, be done to the left foot, too.

Passing the Ball

✓ Easy
Quite Easy
Quite Hard

Here's a trick that'll really keep them guessing!

You'll need:

*A ping-pong ball
Some paper cups
(about ten)*

Stand the paper cups in a pile on one side of the table.

Show everyone the ping-pong ball, and then put it in the top cup of the pile.

Tell everyone to watch carefully. Take the top cup and place it on the other side of the table. Then take the second cup and place it in the middle of the table. Wave your hands over the two cups, and say the magic spell. Move your head as if you are watching the ball move from what was the top cup to the cup that was underneath it.

Look in the cup that was the top cup— the ball isn't there... Pick up the second cup, and show everyone that the ball is there! How on earth did it get there?

The trick:

Prepare the trick beforehand by cutting the bottom out of one cup. Make sure that you put this on the top of the pile.

When you put the ping-pong ball in the top cup, it falls straight through into the second cup. Simple!

The Magic Numb Thumb

Easy
Quite Easy
Quite Hard

You will need:

A carrot
A handkerchief or napkin
Some dressmaking pins (with big heads)

Tell everyone that you can make yourself feel no pain. All you have to do is to put yourself into a trance and that's it.

Close your eyes and gently sway from side to side, while you pretend to put yourself into a pain-killing trance.

Then cover your hand with the napkin and stick the pins into your thumb, one at a time, very slowly.

Smile!

The trick:

Hide a carrot in your hand. When you place the napkin over your hand, make the carrot stick up like a thumb. Then stick the pins into the carrot. You won't feel a thing!

Practice this in front of a mirror before trying it on your friends, to make sure that you hold the carrot so that it really does look like a thumb.

Remember to take the pins out before finishing this trick; otherwise you'll be giving the secret away.

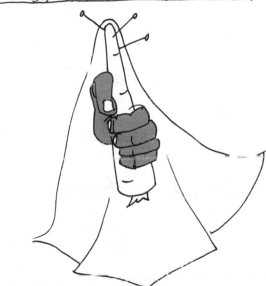

The Great Balloon Burst

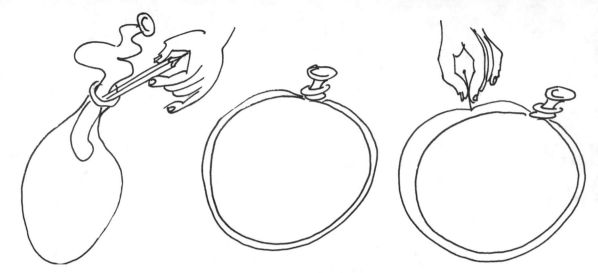

✓ **Easy**
Quite Easy
Quite Hard

This is a very exciting trick that will impress everyone.

You'll need:
Two balloons, the same shape but different colors
A pencil
A pin

Hold up a large balloon. Pick up a pin and tell everyone to watch carefully. Make your movements very slow, so that everyone realizes what you're going to do—burst the balloon!

Toss the balloon up in the air and burst it —but instead of disappearing, the balloon changes color!

The trick:

It's easy, but it needs a little preparation. There is another balloon *inside* the balloon you burst. When the first one pops, you are left holding the second one. It all happens so fast that it looks as if the original balloon has changed color.

This is how you prepare it:

Push one balloon inside the other with the blunt end of the pencil, but make sure the neck of the balloon is sticking out.

Blow up the inside balloon, and tie a knot in the end.

Blow up the outside balloon so that it is a little bigger than the inside one. Tie a knot in the end of this one, too.

When you burst the balloon, try not to push the pin too hard into it, or you may burst both of them!

The Magic Straw

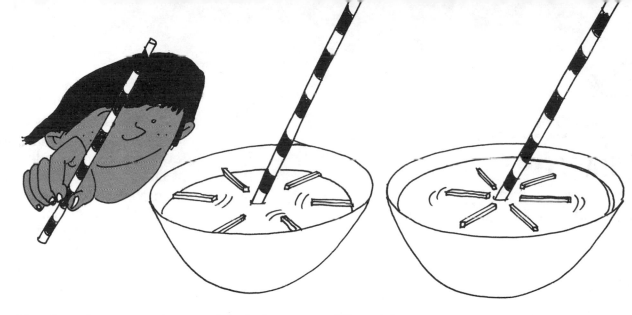

Easy
Quite Easy
Quite Hard

This is a good trick to do with a small group of friends.

You'll need:

A bowl of water
Six used matches
A drinking straw
A bar of soap
Some moist sugar

You float the six matches in a bowl of water and tell everyone that you have special mental powers that can make the matches do what you want.

Dip a straw into the center of the bowl and say, "Hocus-pocus, come to me!"—and the matches will float toward the straw.

Take the straw out of the water, wave it over the matches, and say, "Hocus-pocus, go away!" Dip the straw back into the center of the bowl, and the matches will float away from the straw.

The trick:

Before you do this trick, you will need to prepare the straw. Push one end of the straw into some softened soap, so that some of it is jammed up inside. Then dip the other end into some wet sugar or some honey. Wipe the outside, but make sure some of the substances remain inside, or the trick won't work.

When you dip the sugar end into the water, the matches will move toward the wand— when you dip the soap end in, the matches will move away.

The Mysterious Moving Handkerchief

✓ Easy
Quite Easy
Quite Hard

This is a really simple trick that makes it look as if you've spooked your handkerchief.

You will need:
A handkerchief or a napkin with a hem
A piece of wire

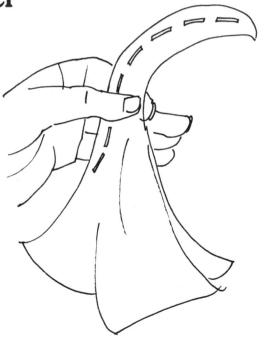

Bewitch your handkerchief by tying a knot in one corner as you murmur a spell. Then tell everyone that the handkerchief knows the name of everyone in the room.

Tell your audience that if someone shouts out a name, the handkerchief will know if it's that person's right name or not.

Someone shouts out her real name. You ask the handkerchief, "Is that her name?" The handkerchief slowly nods.

Someone else shouts out a false name. You ask the handkerchief, "Is that his real name?" The handkerchief hangs limply in your hand.

The trick:

Beforehand you have threaded the wire inside the hem of the handkerchief, from one corner.

You hold the handkerchief loosely in your hand, and it hangs limply down. You squeeze your thumb and forefinger together slightly, and the handkerchief will seem to rise in your hand.

Make the movements slow and deliberate, and they will look more convincing.

Mental Magic

Easy
Quite Easy
Quite Hard

This is a very simple trick, and it works every time. Try it during a meal or during a tea party!

You'll need:

A cup
A fork
A plate
A saucer
A spoon

In a row in front of you, place a cup, a fork, a plate, and a saucer, left to right. They must be in that order.

Ask for a friend to help you do the trick, and make sure that he knows how to spell the names of these objects. Tell him that the trick will not work unless he can get the spelling right.

Then explain that you want him to secretly choose one of the objects. Then you will tap each object with the spoon, once, while he silently spells out the name of the object he has chosen. (He spells out one letter per tap.) When he gets to the last letter, he is to shout, "Stop!"—and your spoon will be pointing to the object he has chosen!

The trick:

The object with the three-letter name is on the left-hand end, the one with the four-letter name next to it, and so on, so that the objects are in sequence according to the number of letters in their names. You begin by choosing any two objects and making a tap on each. Then you must go to the cup (on the left) and tap in the order cup-fork-plate-saucer.

Providing you remember to make **the third tap on the cup,** and follow the sequence, you'll be right every time.

The Number Card

Here's a trick that you can do almost anywhere— provided you've got the number card with you!

Easy
✓ Quite Easy
Quite Hard

You will need:
A copy of this table of numbers on a piece of paper or, better still, a card

1	2	4	8
7	6	13	10
5	3	15	14
3	15	7	13
11	7	6	15
9	10	5	12
13	14	12	11
15	11	14	9

1	2	4	8
7	6	13	10
5	3	15	14
3	15	7	13
11	7	6	15
9	10	5	12
13	14	12	11
15	11	14	9

Ask a friend to mentally pick out a number that is in the table.

Then say to him, "Tell me which vertical column the number appears in. And if it appears in more than one column tell which ones. Then I'll tell you the number you're thinking of."

With amazing speed, you tell him the number!

The trick:

When your friend tells you which columns his number appears in, you quickly add together the numbers that appear in the top row of those columns.

Say your friend says his number appears three times: in the row with 2 at the top, in the row with 4 at the top, and in the row with 8 at the top. Add 2, 4, and 8, and watch his face when you say, "Fourteen!"

The Mind-boggling Mind-reader

✓ **Easy**
Quite Easy
Quite Hard

This trick needs the help of a friend who never leaves the audience!

Telephone!

Tell everyone that you can guess what they are thinking about, because you are such a good magician.

You can prove it. You will go out of the room. While you're out, your audience will choose an object in the room for you to guess. When you come back, you'll be able to tell which object it is.

You do it like this. When you come back in, your assistant will call out lots of objects in the room and you'll be able to tell which object it was that everyone chose.

Of course everyone will think that your assistant is giving you a signal to tell you which object is the right one. They'll watch her very closely, but they'll never be able to find the signal, because she isn't giving you one!

The trick:

You give your assistant the signal! Beforehand you have secretly agreed on a signal: you put your left hand in your pocket, or you scratch your ear. When your assistant sees the signal, she calls out the object that *everyone* chose.
It's so simple!

The Ghost Writer

Easy
Quite Easy
Quite Hard

Here's a trick that will mystify your friends. It's all done with the help of a friendly "ghost"!

You'll need:

A pencil with a soft lead
A cube of sugar
A cup of water

Tell your friend to write her initial on the sugar cube with the pencil. Make sure that it is written very clearly, as your friendly ghost can't see very well...

Then pick up the sugar cube, and drop it into the cup of water.

Take your friend's hand, and hold it over the cup. Say the magic words.

Turn your friend's hand over—and the letter she wrote is on her hand!

The trick:

When you pick up the sugar cube to put it in the cup, make sure that you press your finger firmly onto the place where she has written her initial.

This will transfer the writing to your finger.

Then when you take your friend by the hand, press that finger into your friend's palm. The writing will be transferred to her hand.

The Magnetic Hand

✓ Easy
Quite Easy
Quite Hard

With practice you can pick up a whole deck of cards in one hand, without holding onto them!

You will need:

*A deck of cards
A ring
A toothpick
A sheet of paper*

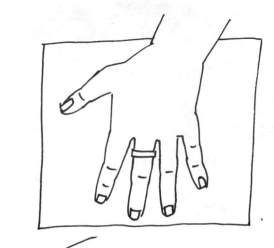

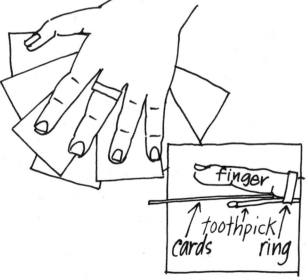

Tell everyone that you can make your hand magnetic, so that things stick to it whenever you want them to.

Put your hand (with the fingers spread out) on a sheet of paper and try to pick it up— but of course you won't be able to.

Pick up the deck of cards and show them to everyone to convince them that they are perfectly ordinary cards (which of course they are).

Then put your hand down on the table again, with your fingers spread out, and begin to push the cards under it, one at a time.

When you've pushed enough under it, slowly lift your hand—they're stuck to it!

Put your hand down on the table again, and pull them out one at a time, so that you don't give away your secret.

The trick:

Before you begin this trick, put on a ring and push a toothpick underneath it. The first two cards go between the toothpick and your finger. The other cards go between the first two cards and your hand.

62

The Magic Talking Card

Easy
Quite Easy
Quite Hard

So you don't think that playing-cards can talk? They can if you're a magician!

You'll need:

A normal deck of cards

Pick up the deck and shuffle the cards. Then place the deck in your left hand, with the fingers flat. Hold out your right hand, palm up, and ask someone from your audience to take half the cards and put them onto your right hand. Keep all the cards face down.

Tell your friend to take any card she likes from either of the piles.

Then tell her to rest that card on top of the pile in your right hand. Count up to five, and then pick the card up and hold it to your ear.

You listen carefully, nod, and then tell your friend that the card has told you a secret— the name of the top card in your right hand.

Your friend turns over the top card in your right hand—and you're correct!

The trick:

Beforehand, you must secretly remember the top card in the deck. When you shuffle the deck, be careful to keep that card on the top all the time. When the person from the audience puts half the deck into your right hand, the top card is now on top of the right pile.

If your friend decides to take the very top card in your right hand, you can make the trick even more impressive. Tell her to place it on top of the pile in your other hand, and then hold the card that was underneath it to your ear. You can then tell your friend which card she actually chose!

Logical Magic

✓ **Easy**
Quite Easy
Quite Hard

This trick is easy, but it's still amazing!

You'll need:
Two coins—a nickel and a dime

You ask two members of your audience to come up and help you do this trick.

First tell them that you're going out of the room for a moment. As soon as you leave, one of them must decide to be a liar, and one of them must decide to be the truth-teller—and the liar must *always* lie, and the truth-teller must *always* tell the truth. Then each one of them must pick up a coin. It doesn't matter which coin they pick up.

When you come back you're going to tell them which one has which coin.

Then you go out of the room.

When you come back you ask one of them "Has the liar got the dime?"

If the person you ask says "Yes," then the other person has the dime. But if the person you ask says "No," then that person has the dime.

The trick:

Well, there is no trick here, except logic. And if you can work out the logic behind it, then you're a genius!

Scratching

*Here's a trick that
is hardly a trick at
all, and it needs
no special
practice
beforehand.*

Easy
Quite Easy
Quite Hard

You'll need:

*A table covered
with a tablecloth
A glass
Two dimes
One quarter*

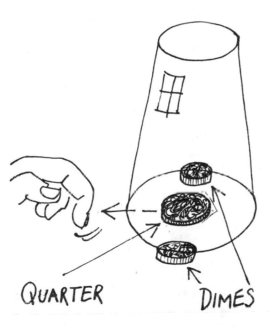

QUARTER   DIMES

Place two dimes on the tablecloth, and
then stand the glass upside down on top
of them. This should leave a small gap
between the glass and the tablecloth.

Tell your audience that you're going to
place the quarter underneath the glass
and then magically make it come out to
you, without touching it.

Show everyone the quarter—and
even let one or two people hold it to make
sure that there is nothing attached...

Lift up the glass, and place the coin
underneath it.

Then you scratch gently on the tablecloth.
The coin begins to move toward you, and
out from under the glass!

The trick:

Keep scratching toward you, not too far
away from the glass. This will make the
coin move along.

More Mental Magic

SQUEEZE
SQUEEZE
SQUEEZE

THREE!

✓ **Easy**
Quite Easy
Quite Hard

Here's another trick that uses your magical mental powers, this time to tell your audience what numbers they have decided to get you to guess.

You'll need:
A friend

Tell everyone that your mental powers are strong today, and that you feel ready to use them. You're going to use your abilities to read your friend's mind.

Tell your audience that you're going out of the room. While you're out, they should decide on three numbers under 30 that they want you to guess. They must tell those numbers to your friend.

You go out of the room, and then come back. You turn your friend so that he faces the audience (they can see that he isn't telling you the numbers), and stand behind him. You place a finger lightly on both of his temples explaining that this helps you

to pick up his thoughts, and then look serious.

In a moment you call out the numbers!

The trick:
What your friend does is this:

He puts his back teeth firmly together, and then, for each number, squeezes them a little tighter. This makes a muscle in his temple bulge out. If the number is 15, he squeezes his teeth together one time, then pauses, and then squeezes them five times. If the number is a zero, he relaxes his jaw a little, so that the muscle doesn't bulge at all, and gives a tiny sniff.

Your Magic Assistant

This trick is so simple that it's hard to believe it actually works. But it does—every time!

Easy
Quite Easy
Quite Hard

You'll need:

A table
A paper cup
A pen
Coins (preferably from your audience)

Before you begin the trick, explain to your audience that you will now transfer your magic mind-reading powers to your assistant for this trick.

Place both hands on her head and screw your face up in concentration.

Get some coins from your audience: a nickel, a dime, a quarter, and a penny.

Then tell everyone that your powers are strong enough for your assistant to know what coin will be under the cup that you have on the table in front of you.

Your assistant then goes out of the room.

While she is out, you place one of the coins under the cup, and then put the rest in your pocket.

You call your assistant in. She immediately says which coin is under the cup!

a penny

spot turned away

The trick:

Beforehand, you make a tiny dot on the side of the cup. When your assistant comes in, she looks for the dot. If it is in front of her, the coin is a nickel. If it's to the left, it's a dime. If it's to the right, it's a quarter, and if she can't see it at all because it's on the other side, away from her, it's the penny.

You can do this trick several times, and the audience will still not guess how it's done!

The Floating Egg

✓ Easy
Quite Easy
Quite Hard

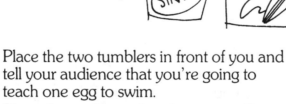

This trick relies on a little science.

You'll need:
2 tumblers with water in them
5 large spoonfuls of sugar
2 (raw) eggs in their shells
A waterproof marker pen

Place the two tumblers in front of you and tell your audience that you're going to teach one egg to swim.

Show the audience that the eggs really can't swim yet. Put them into one of the tumblers one at a time, and watch them sink to the bottom.

Now get someone from the audience to write on one of the eggs the word "swim," and on the other "sink."

Wave your hands over the "swim" egg, and place it on the table in front of you. Tell your audience to watch it carefully to make sure that you don't switch it.

Then pick up the "sink" egg, and put it back into the first tumbler. It sinks. Pick up the "swim" egg and place it in the second tumbler. It floats on the surface!

If you like, you can then take them out of the water, and break them open to show that they are the same inside.

PLAIN WATER

Both eggs will sink

SUGAR WATER

Both eggs will float

PLAIN WATER

SUGAR WATER

DON'T MIX THE GLASSES UP — YOU'LL SPOIL THE TRICK.

We're off for a swim

Well don't get wet!

The trick:

Beforehand, you fill one of the tumblers with warm water and put the sugar into it. Stir the sugar around until it has dissolved.

Next, make sure that the trick will work. Try putting one of the eggs into this tumbler — it should float. If it doesn't, add a bit more sugar to the water and stir it thoroughly.

Easy — and very scientific!

The Floating Sugar Cube

Bloop!

✓ Easy
Quite Easy
Quite Hard

You'll need:

5 sugar cubes
A cup
Some strong,
recently made tea
Some milk

You will show everyone that you can make a sugar cube float on top of a cup of tea.

You place a cup of tea on the table in front of you where everyone can see, and then show them a cube of sugar that you are holding in your hand. Carefully you place the sugar cube on the surface of the tea — and it floats!

After a few moments, you point to the cup and say commandingly, "Sink!" — and it does!

The trick:

Beforehand, you stack four sugar cubes on top of each other in the cup. Wet the

surfaces slightly so that the cubes stick together to form a pillar.

Make the tea, and leave it to cool a little. If it's too hot, the trick won't work. Don't let it get cold, though, or the disappearing act won't work!

THE SECRET REVEALED →

Pour the tea out into the cup, and add milk. The tea should just cover the top sugar cube, so that it can't be seen.

When you place the sugar cube on the surface of the tea, you're actually putting it carefully on top of the pillar of cubes. The warm tea will gradually dissolve the cubes, and the one on top will gradually sink beneath the surface. Just before it does, wave your hand and command it to sink.

You will need to practice this beforehand to see how long it takes for the cubes to dissolve. The hotter the tea the faster they will dissolve.

Picking the Number

Easy
Quite Easy
Quite Hard

This trick needs the help of an assistant—but it'll fool everyone else!

You'll need:

Some paper
A pencil
A dried pea or a very small bean
A big glass bowl or dish

You call out for an assistant from the audience and explain that he is going to help you in the trick.

You explain that you will now go out of the room. While you're away, everyone is going to decide on a number—any number from 1 to 20. Your assistant will write the number on a piece of paper, crinkle it up into a ball, and put it in the bowl. Then everyone will give lots of other numbers, and your assistant will write those numbers down on pieces of paper, crinkle each one up into a ball, and put it into the bowl.

When you come back, everyone must think very hard of that first number. If they think hard enough, you'll be able to read their minds, and pick out the correct piece of paper from the bowl.

When you come back into the room, someone will say that you're cheating— the piece of paper is the one at the bottom! So call that person up and ask her to give the papers a really good stir. You'll be able to pick it anyway!

GENTLY SQUEEZE

The trick:

When your assistant crinkles the first piece of paper up, he puts the dried bean into the ball. When you search for the paper, you gently squeeze each ball—the one you are looking for will have the bean in the middle!

When you smooth out the paper, make sure that you secretly remove the bean before anyone can see it—hide it in your hand.

The Magic Bottle

This trick needs a little preparation, but it works every time, and will mystify your friends.

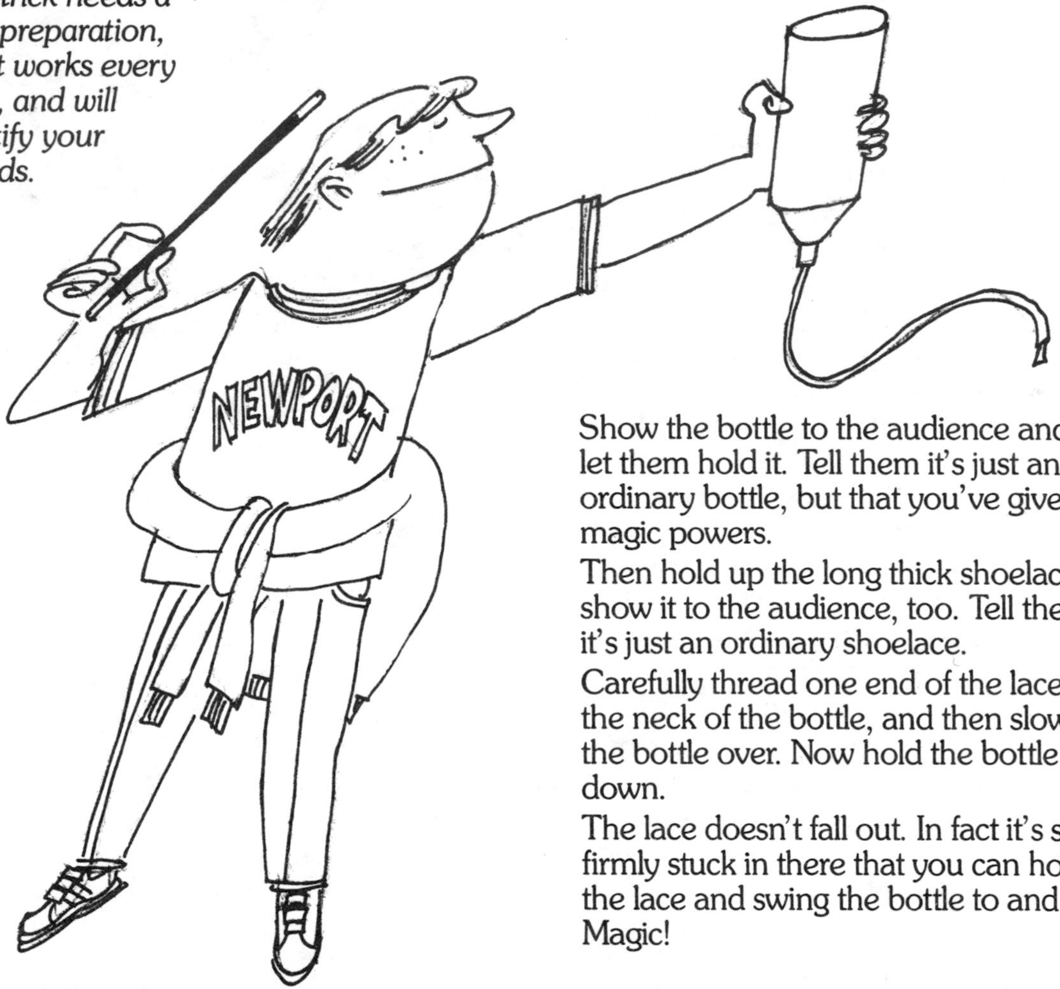

✓ **Easy**
   Quite Easy
   Quite Hard

You'll need:

*An empty opaque plastic bottle (the neck should be quite narrow)
A long thick shoelace
A cork from a bottle*

Show the bottle to the audience and even let them hold it. Tell them it's just an ordinary bottle, but that you've given it magic powers.

Then hold up the long thick shoelace and show it to the audience, too. Tell them that it's just an ordinary shoelace.

Carefully thread one end of the lace into the neck of the bottle, and then slowly tip the bottle over. Now hold the bottle upside down.

The lace doesn't fall out. In fact it's so firmly stuck in there that you can hold onto the lace and swing the bottle to and fro. Magic!

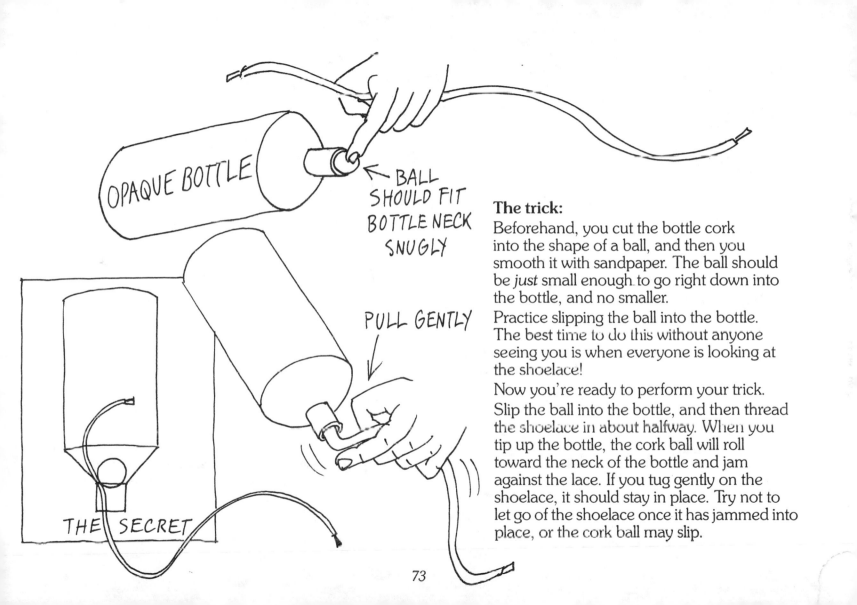

OPAQUE BOTTLE

← BALL SHOULD FIT BOTTLE NECK SNUGLY

PULL GENTLY

THE SECRET

The trick:

Beforehand, you cut the bottle cork into the shape of a ball, and then you smooth it with sandpaper. The ball should be *just* small enough to go right down into the bottle, and no smaller.

Practice slipping the ball into the bottle. The best time to do this without anyone seeing you is when everyone is looking at the shoelace!

Now you're ready to perform your trick.

Slip the ball into the bottle, and then thread the shoelace in about halfway. When you tip up the bottle, the cork ball will roll toward the neck of the bottle and jam against the lace. If you tug gently on the shoelace, it should stay in place. Try not to let go of the shoelace once it has jammed into place, or the cork ball may slip.

Raising a Friend in the Air

This is a really amazing trick that isn't at all complicated. But be warned—it's quite hard to make it look convincing!

Easy
Quite Easy
✓ **Quite Hard**

You will need:
Two identical pairs of shoes (one of them being worn by a friend)
Two sticks
A sheet
A bench

Tell everyone that it's really very easy to make someone float into the air, and that you will show them how.

Call up three people from the audience. Get two of them to hold up the sheet, and the third friend to go behind it and lie down on the bench.

As soon as your friend is lying down, the two helpers cover him with the sheet so that it hangs down on either side.

You stand behind the boy lying down and wave your hands, saying the magic spell. Slowly the boy rises in the air, still lying down!

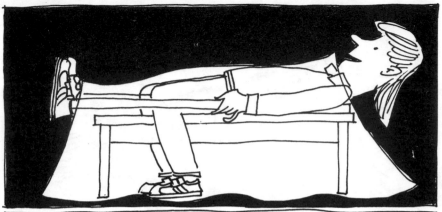

BENCH →

The trick:

You have to practice this trick often before you try it.

All three of your helpers have been "trained" beforehand. The two who hold the sheet will have to be in on the trick, as they will see what is going on!

Before the trick begins, attach one of the pairs of shoes to the sticks as shown in the illustration. Then hide them under the bench which you have covered with the sheet.

When the trick begins, the third friend places the two sticks with the shoes tied onto the end on the bench, so that the shoes stick out. Then he lies down on the bench but with his knees bent and his own feet still on the ground.

When you say the magic spell, he grasps hold of the two sticks, and, holding them firmly, slowly stands up, while still bending back as if he is lying down.

Your friend will have to practice standing up without giving the secret away, and he will have to learn how to hold the sticks so that they stay level.

If it's done properly, it will amaze everyone watching!